THE CHURCH IN HINDON

To Mum

Wishing you a happy Christmas and a great New Year – 2001.

Derek & Jean

Cover photos, R. Dewhurst, 1995.

The Church in Hindon

Richard Dewhurst

HINDON PUBLISHING

First Published in 2000 by
Hindon Publishing
Tanswell, High Street, Hindon, Salisbury, Wiltshire SP3 6DJ

Design and typesetting by Ex Libris Press, Bradford on Avon

Printed by Cromwell Press, Trowbridge

This work has been commissioned by the Parochial Church Council (PCC) of the Church of St. John the Baptist, Hindon.

© Richard Dewhurst; © illustrations and photographs as indicated.

A CIP catalogue record of this book is available from the British Library.

ISBN 0 9531586 2 4

CONTENTS

Foreword, by the Revd. Richard Wren		7
Acknowledgements		9
History	Introduction	11
	Earliest times	11
	The coming of Christianity	13
	At 1066	15
	The foundation of Hindon	16
	The development of Hindon chapel	21
	Reformation to Restoration	24
	The 18th Century	33
	Towards a new parish and church	37
	Nonconformism	42
	Hindon church in modern times	45
Hindon old chapel - a description		49
The Church of St. John the Baptist, Hindon		52
Appendix A. Chaplains / curates of old Hindon chapel		58
Appendix B. Vicars of Hindon		60
References		62

Foreword

This booklet was conceived as a fitting marker for the Hindon millennial celebrations. Although there have been previous booklets about Hindon, there has been none that so fully describes the church. We have also approached the history of Hindon in a different way, and in a manner which befits the celebration of 2000 years of Christianity, by tracing the history of the development of the faith in the village and the surrounding area.

Apart from looking afresh at old sources, the author has had the advantage of major new studies written since the last booklet on Hindon in 1979. These have helped him correct some commonly held assumptions of the time, not least that the present church of 1870-71 replaced a Tudor building. But records of the medieval and Tudor periods are so scant that he has had to suggest a pattern of worship and events from known practice generally.

It is almost impossible to express the extent of our thanks to Richard Dewhurst. He lives only a stone's throw from the church and has been painstaking in his research and energy over nearly two years. In his investigations he has revealed more material than could be included here and that has been deposited in the village archives. I am sure that his lively work will be considered as definitive for many years to come.

I hope that you not only purchase this booklet as a souvenir of our celebrations (or, if you are a visitor, as a reminder of your visit) but that you also actually read it. This is not just a history of a place; it is more than that, it is a record of people's lives, their

The Church in Hindon

decisions, their passions and their beliefs. All those who live here, those who can trace their families back through generations in the village, or who have moved in recently, are inheritors of those who laboured, loved and died here over the centuries. Their responsibility, to create a safe and loving community based on a firm faith in Christ, now passes to us and the symbol of that, our church, stands proudly at the head of the High Street.

The body of the church proclaims a living faith on earth and the spire points to heaven.

Richard Wren
Parish Priest

Author's acknowledgements

My sincere thanks are due to many people. To Tom Blake of Tilshead, who first pointed me towards the sources and who read my text. To the staff of the Wilts. and Swindon Record Office in Trowbridge, and in particular to Stephen Hobbs. To Pamela Colman, late Sandell Librarian of the Wiltshire Archaeological and Natural History Society (WANHS) in Devizes, and to the Curator of Winchester Cathedral, John Hardacre. To Tony Claydon, for access to East Knoyle vestry records, and to Dr. Richard Godfrey, diocesan organ advisor, for his assessment of the organ.

In Hindon, I could not have got by without Heather Bull, for reminiscences, inquiries, and access to pioneering notes on Hindon's history made by her late father Edward Jerrim, previously used but not acknowledged, that saved me from a long sentence in the PRO. Nor without Geoffrey Curtis, for access to vestry records and for patient coaching in church organisation and parochial changes; nor Oliver Lodge, for use of village archives, his local knowledge and his stringent lawyer's correction of my text.

Of others too numerous to list in full I am indebted variously for introductions, suggestions, reminiscences, inquiries, documents and photographs to the late Basil Bevis, Paul Britton, Linda Coleman of Wessex Archaeology, Pam Collis, Joan Giles, Peggy Jones née Pitman, Rosemary MacDonald, Mary Muhlethaler, Geoffrey Richards, John Snook and Anne Spanton.

But none of this would have got anywhere without the beautiful typing of Philippa Cawthorne and Jules Attlee.

HISTORY

Introduction

Hindon, in the south west corner of Wiltshire, is an oddity among English villages. By the standards of most of them, the foundation neither of Hindon nor of its church is particularly ancient. It seems certain that there was no sizeable settlement here until the years around 1220, when a Bishop of Winchester, whose see owned the land, planted a market borough along the line of the present High Street, within the eastern boundary of East Knoyle parish. Church followed commerce. At times the little town achieved some prosperity by the standards of its day, based more on its geographical position than on any native resource, but its church did not achieve parish status independent of East Knoyle until 1869. Today, the village does not differ too much in plan or size from that distant one-off foundation. It now lies just off the main trunk roads, by the same distance and in the same direction, as it did in prehistoric times.

Earliest times

No Hindon dog walker or passing back-packer can fail to notice that this landscape has a very ancient history. Two to three miles to the NW and W lie two Neolithic long barrows, suggesting significant communities of the earliest farmers existing over many generations, preserving their ancestors' bones in elaborate graves, maybe five or six thousand years ago. The area can be said to be littered with later Bronze Age barrows ('tumuli' on OS maps), tombs of the rich and powerful. From the Iron Age (c.800 BC to the Roman period) there are about 16 hill forts within 10 miles. Many traces of ancient field systems can still be seen, the nearest NW, W and SW of Hindon in the present fields towards the A350.[1] The place that is now Hindon was also just off major prehistoric communications routes. The Great Ridgeway, perhaps the oldest, passes $2\frac{1}{2}$ miles to the N on its way from Imber and beyond through Pertwood and down the A350 to the Dorset coast, and a subsidiary track probably led south from it through the present line of Hindon High Street. The Harroway passed from Stonehenge along the line of the present A303 at Chicklade, and the Grovely Ridgeway ran along Great Ridge to the N.[2] Two Roman roads, from Old Sarum to the Mendips and from Badbury Rings to Bath passed nearby. There can be no doubt that people have lived in this general area, farmed intensively, traded and worshipped their gods or ancestors from time out of mind.

But not, it is often said, in Hindon itself, and 1220 is usually given as the date of first occupation. However the place-name, although the earliest written record of it known to the writer (as 'Hinedun') is not earlier than 1224, is clearly derived from Anglo-Saxon. Scholars tell us that the 'don' element comes from the Old English 'dun,' meaning a hill or down. They speculate that 'hin' may come from 'higna,' genetive plural of an OE word meaning a household, ecclesiastical or secular.[3] This, if correct, could suggest that there was a household here, or that somebody lived here who belonged to a household elsewhere.

The coming of Christianity

There may, therefore, have been something here in Anglo-Saxon times. Given the line of the present High Street and that, in medieval times a track on the line of the present B3089 from Wilton to Willoughby Hedge crossed it in the present village, it could be that the latter road is also very old and that something, perhaps a building or two, stood at or near the present cross-roads. However, since excavation below occupied buildings is seldom a viable proposition, it is doubtful if we shall ever know.

The coming of Christianity

To date there is no evidence to show whether or not Christianity gained any foothold in this part of Wiltshire in Roman times (AD43 – c.420). In other parts of the county there are a few isolated and ambiguous archaeological finds to suggest that some big landowners could have introduced some form of Christian worship, possibly 'syncretized' with pagan forms.[4,5]

After the pagan Anglo-Saxon occupation of large parts of England, Christian missions from Rome began with Augustine's evangelization of Kent from 597. Thereafter progress was piecemeal, kingdom by little kingdom, and intermittent. Wessex received a series of continental bishops sent from Rome: first Birinus, a Benedictine who baptised King Cynegils in 635 and was given a new see at Dorchester-on-Thames. In about 662 King Cenwalh established Wine as bishop in Winchester, replacing Dorchester. This became a vast see covering Hampshire and most of Wessex, and was the centre from which these parts began systematically to be converted.

The Saxons are not noted for their record keeping skills and the evolution of diocesan organisation is even now not entirely clear. It seems that Winchester was soon broken up. Parts west of Selwood transferred to a new see at Sherborne in the early 8th century, and others to Ramsbury about 909, covering Wiltshire and parts of Berkshire and Oxfordshire.[6] Hindon would probably have come within its bounds; at the Conquest this certainly seems to have been the case.[7] Some of these sees had been underendowed, and in William I's reign Ramsbury and Sherborne were reunited under Bishop Herman of Sherborne. The London Synod of 1075 directed that all episcopal seats should be moved from villages to cities, and Herman's see was transferred to Salisbury, then on the hill that we now know as Old Sarum. The final act of reorganisation was the removal of the cathedral and bishop's palace down to the riverside meadows at New Salisbury from 1220, at exactly the same time that Hindon was being founded.

None of this helps us to say when this precise area was Christianized. In the early missionary period bishops were not administrators but evangelical and often itinerant preachers, who attached themselves to kings or lords, hoping that by converting them the message would spread down to their people, and that these patrons would build them a wooden church and endow them and their clergy. This was the start of lay patronage. The reverse of the coin was that these patrons had complete control; they could say how things were to be organised, and could move the clergy and even the church buildings from place to place. It took some centuries for the parochial system to develop and provide the clergy with a regular establishment.

Later, much evangelizing was done from religious houses.

Secular (non monastic) churches from which conversion of an area radiated were known as minsters (of various grades). Minsters in this area are recorded at Warminster (8 miles), Heytesbury (6 miles), Mere (6 miles), and Gillingham, Dorset ($7\frac{1}{2}$ miles).[9,10] There was also the great nunnery at Shaftesbury (7 miles), endowed by Alfred (r. 871-899). We do not know whether any of these establishments founded the church at East Knoyle, whose parish included Hindon, or when. The earliest surviving record of the place-name for Knoyle, as Cnugel, dates from 948, but that tells us little.[11] There was, however, a church in Anglo-Saxon times. In the present church, "parts of the walls of the nave and of the western part of the chancel remain from a pre-Conquest church."[12]

At 1066

The great Domesday survey of 1086 assessed the value of the manor of East Knoyle on the eve of the Norman Conquest.[13] It reported:

> "The King (William I) holds Knoyle. Aeleva held it before 1066. It paid tax for 30 hides. Land for 15 ploughs. In lordship $17\frac{1}{2}$ hides; 5 ploughs, 10 slaves.
> 16 villagers, 10 smallholders and 18 cottagers with 10 ploughs. Meadow, 15 acres; pasture 1 league long and $\frac{1}{2}$ league wide, woodland $\frac{1}{2}$ league long and as wide.
> The value was £28; now £30.
> Gilbert has 1 hide of this land. 3 smallholders are there. Value 7s 6d."[14]

It is difficult to interpret this. Originally the hide was the basic

Anglo-Saxon land division sufficient to support the average peasant, but it varied geographically and according to the productivity of the land. Records are very scant and we shall all be long gone before scholars finish discussing how many acres went to a hide in any one area. In Wessex a figure of 40 is often quoted, but where documents such as Domesday give any correlation at all, a lower and variable figure seems to emerge.[15,16] We cannot, therefore, say how much of Knoyle manor was cultivated, or whether this extended to the present Hindon on its edge. It does, however, in the lady Aeleva and Gilbert, give us the first personal names associated with this place.

The foundation of Hindon

The foundation of Hindon may not be vastly ancient, but unlike most older English villages it can identify its founder. Bishop Sir Peter des Roches, or de Rochys, or in Latin texts Petrus de Rupibus, was a native of Poitou, south of the Loire or Anjou, north of it, then part of the possessions of the English crown. He served there as knight and clerk under Richard Coeur de Lion, and became a chamberlain at his court. When John succeeded in 1199, des Roches came to England, continued in the royal service and became a close friend, confidant and fixer for the King. He travelled with John and conducted negotiations for him abroad, in reward for which John promoted his consecration as Bishop of Winchester in 1205. He closely supported John in his struggle with Pope Innocent III over ecclesiastical appointments, was left in effective charge of the realm when John campaigned in France in 1213 and 1214, and stood by him during the struggles with the barons that resulted

The foundation of Hindon

in the signing of Magna Carta in 1215.

When John died in 1216 the barons were still in arms against him, and a French army was in rather aimless control of the south east and East Anglia. The royal party gathered at Gloucester, and it was des Roches, one of John's executors, who, in a makeshift coronation ceremony, placed a plain gold circlet on the nine-year-old Henry III's head, the royal regalia not being to hand (it was in the Wash). He became the boy's guardian and tutor. In 1217 he was one of the captains of a royalist force that marched to relieve other royalist troops besieged in the castle at Lincoln by rebels and French in the town. On a solo reconnaissance into the castle des Roches noticed a blocked-up gateway that, when later breached, let the royalists into the town to scatter the much larger rebel forces. This effectively ended the French occupation.

In the confused and factious politics of Henry's early personal reign des Roches' influence declined. He went on the Sixth Crusade 1228-31, and acted as mediator between the squabbling Emperor Frederick II and Pope Gregory IX. Returning with a vast reputation as an independent international statesman, he became from 1232 the motive force of an administration packed with Poitevin relatives and cronies. A rise of reformist and nationalist feeling in the English church led to his fall, and in 1235 he left to offer his sword to Gregory IX in Italy. He died in 1238; his tomb is in Winchester Cathedral (plate 1).[17,18,19]

This formidable warrior priest, cultivated, subtle, arrogant, a ruthlessly efficient administrator, not at all English, was one of the most competent men of his time. There is no reason to doubt his conventional piety. He was an assiduous founder of churches and religious houses in England and the Holy Land, and paid much attention to the prosperity of his bishopric.

One of the simplest ways of increasing one's wealth and encouraging trade in the 13th century was by setting up a market. A licence had to be obtained from the King. One erected dwellings for the stall holders on some frequented route, with what were called burgage plots behind, and drew rents from the tenants and market dues from the profits. In modern jargon, many jobs were created. Bishop Peter himself founded or enlarged markets on Winchester land at Downton (1208), Overton, Hampshire (by 1213), Newtown in Beauclere (1218), and Hindon (by 1220).[20]

Why Hindon? It will be noticed that Winchester, Downton, Hindon and Taunton, where the bishops had a large manor and castle, are more or less on an east-west line. Travelling between their existing manors the bishops with their retinues and stewards must have safaried more or less along the line of the present B3089 through Hindon to Willoughby Hedge, and Bishop Peter would have been familiar with the point where it crossed the present High Street.

Why choose it for a borough and market? *The Victoria County History/Wiltshire (VCH/Wilts)* suggests "perhaps ...... Hindon was built as far as possible from the rival centres of Mere and Shaftesbury, and as near as possible to the villages of the upper Nadder Valley and to those lying between the market towns of Warminster and Wilton."[21] This would imply that the track leading from the Wylye and the Great Ridgeway was a viable road still in some usage, and could suggest that the crossing with the east-west route was not entirely a 'green field site.'

The foundation of Hindon

Another recommendation was water. In a cloudburst it pours off the surrounding downs to the Dene at the lowest point in the village, as modern residents know to their cost. Perhaps the bishop's party, in transit one day, got caught in such a storm and des Roches' keen eye saw the possibility of sinking wells to trap this flow. Sure enough, in 1220-1 the bishopric paid for the sinking of an 84 foot well (21s.) with a rope and an iron-bound bucket (1s.). Beresford comments "Like Truth it may one day be found at the bottom of a well."[22]

The town was laid out across a wide street (now the High Street) running NW from the parish south boundary. Narrow burgage plots ran behind the houses, and lanes between them led to the fields behind, like the bones of a kipper. Despite intrusions and divisions this layout can still be traced on the ground. A footpath (Back Way) runs behind the burgage plots to the west almost the whole length of the High Street. Had Hindon continued to develop and expand as Salisbury did, this path would have become a street and plots the other side of it would have eventually produced a grid plan, as in Salisbury.

The weekly market began almost immediately after Hindon's plantation. The tenants would have pitched their stalls in the street outside their cottages. By 1220-1 Hindon was designated a 'burgus' or borough (as such it began to send two members to Parliament in 1448, and it was an occasional venue for JP's quarter sessions from 1530). Peter des Roches was partly responsible for enforcing nationally an earlier, largely disregarded, royal edict that markets should be held on a weekday so that everybody could worship on Sunday.[23] In earlier times markets were often held on Sundays, the only day the poor peasants were free from toil to buy or sell necessities. How they fitted this in after enforcement of the edict is, of course, not recorded, but Bishop Peter, true to his own precept, fixed Hindon's (and Downton's) market for a Thursday, and there it remained until its demise in the early 1880s.

More important than markets in the early middle ages were fairs. Markets were weekly affairs in towns, essential to their sustenance and survival in the days before permanent shops. Fairs were usually annual or biannual events attracting visitors from further afield, sometimes from abroad. They occurred on two or three days round saints' days or other religious festivals, contained an element of celebration and merry-making, and in many cases were the remote descendants of pagan festivals. Medieval kings subjected them to the same regulation as markets. A fair at Hindon at Michaelmas (29th September) was granted to the Bishop of Winchester in 1219, a square marked out and a market cross and a building for merchants erected.[24] Probably due to the success of this, in 1331 Edward III replaced it by the grant of two annual three-day fairs, at Ascension (moveable between 30th April and 3rd June) and St. Luke's Day (18th October).[25] St. Luke was the dedicatee of the chapel in Hindon before the present patron saint, John the Baptist.[26]

The crossroads between the present Lamb Inn and the Grosvenor Arms is still called 'The Square,' and if it is imagined without the cluster of buildings round the present Post Office stores, the cottages on the north side of Salisbury Road, Steeple Close and the grassed area in front of the Lamb Inn, which are probably later intrusions, a considerable open space is suggested which is almost certainly the fair's site. None of the medieval buildings appear to survive, but the visitor today can walk the present village and, to a considerable extent, see the fossilised ground plan of a small medieval market town that serviced the surrounding area.

Apart from Hindon Fair, there was also a major sheep fair on Cold Berwick Hill (GR ST 922341), the origins of which may have been very ancient. This happened around 6th November, the feast of St. Leonard. Although it was in the parish of Berwick St. Leonard, Hindon must have been involved. This part of Wiltshire is interlaced with drove routes.[27] The wide verges of at least five of the eight roads radiating from Hindon suggest that they served as drove routes. Berwick Fair, whenever it began, had the usual astonishing longevity. First recorded in the late 13th century, it survived until 1867.[28] Even in 1833, when the railways were just beginning to threaten the droving trade, the fair penned 14,000 sheep.[29] Many of these would have passed through Hindon. The place must have been filled with bleating and dust, and strange, outlandish drovers stalking about the place, alarming the local citizenry and trying to steal their chickens.

The development of Hindon chapel

Winchester episcopal accounts for 1223-4 record expenditure "in the building of the chapel of Hinedun on the order of the bishop 13s 4d." [30] There may have been other money from elsewhere, but this low figure may suggest a small wooden structure. It is highly likely it was on the church's present site. There is a strong possibility that its dedication was originally to St. Michael Archangel; the grant of a fair to Hindon at Michaelmas (p.20) suggests it. In the middle ages fairs, with their connotations of festival and holiday, were commonly held on the patron saint's day, and rents and dues were often paid at the same time. It is notable that two entries in a register of transfers of land in Hindon that probably pre-date 1300 stipulate that new lessees are to pay rent "annually on the feast of St. Michael Archangel.[31] It is said that many early dedications to St. Michael were of buildings on hilltops or rising ground; this would fit with a chapel having been on the present site from the start.

The renewed charter of 1331 for fairs at Ascension and St. Luke's Day (p.20) suggests that the dedication was changed (not an uncommon occurrence in the middle ages) at that time. Certainly, the chapel was dedicated to St. Luke by 1553.[32]

The see of Winchester, as lords of the manor of East Knoyle, provided the chapel in the tradition of the pioneering churches (p.14), but of course was not responsible for the cure of souls in Hindon, which was by then in Salisbury diocese. Winchester seems to have provided no endowment for the chapel or for a priest, and the rector of East Knoyle became responsible. The chapel "was presumably poorly served by the rector and at least in the later 14th century, when the inhabitants had to attend their parish church (East Knoyle), almost certainly closed."[33] If this is correct, one wonders whether this was an effect of the Black Death. The poorer clergy of Wiltshire were particularly badly hit by the plague in 1349, presumably from dutifully attending the dying, and if a priest and half the inhabitants of Hindon were dead it is difficult to see how services there could have been carried on. A folk memory of those bad times may have been enshrined in a petition to the Crown

The development of Hindon Chapel

two centuries later (p.26) about the straits of Hindon chapel which recounted the difficulty of getting to Sunday worship in East Knoyle,

> "which is distant two miles and more from Hindon and the road between the two so impeded in winter with waters and streams which grow to such depth and breadth that the inhabitants of the borough and their families are unable to cross them almost throughout the whole season . . . ."[34]

A bishop's register of 1393 lists a "William Stok, chaplain of Hindon", so church activity must have recommenced locally by then.[35] The chapel, refounded and probably partly rebuilt (in common with many derelict Wiltshire churches and churchyards at this time), reopened as a 'chapel-of-ease' to East Knoyle, with a chaplain appointed by its rector. It was customary for a rector to retain some control over a chapel-of-ease in his parish by keeping the right of, usually, burial in his own churchyard. In Hindon's case it was marriages that the chaplain could not conduct (although, for reasons unknown, a few were registered between 1608 and 1651).

The papal licence that granted the rector appointment of the chaplain of Hindon stipulated that if he failed to appoint, the inhabitants of Hindon should do so. In the 15th century they endowed the chapel with buildings and land to produce a revenue, and in return received sole right of appointment of the chaplain. The rector of East Knoyle, however, continued to receive the tithes of the chapelry,[36] an arrangement that accentuated the contrast between East Knoyle, a fairly wealthy living, and Hindon, where the chaplains (sometimes referred to as curates) seem most of the time to have lived near the poverty line.

Evidence of the physical appearance of the medieval Hindon chapel, which was swept away in 1869 for the building of the present church, is considered in the separate section (p.49). Suffice it to say here that it was a small hall-like structure with no apparent division of nave and chancel, and a tower on the south side. In common with parish churches of this time, the congregation would mostly have stood, though seating at the side walls would be provided for the old and sick ('the weak to the wall'). It would have been, in winter, very dark, and possibly decorated with rather lurid wall paintings, if anybody in the town could paint. The chapel would be used not only for worship, but for chapel and vestry meetings, any village business, perhaps even as a market in bad weather. Some Wiltshire churches or churchyards were, despite episcopal discouragement, also used for 'church ales,' or drinking celebrations, and even dancing to celebrate certain events, for example patronal festivals. These were an important source of income to poor churches. The parallel with modern fund-raising events, although they may be more decorous today, will not be lost on the reader.

Reformation to Restoration

The remainder of the 15th and the beginning of the 16th centuries have left no records that might shed light on the condition of Hindon chapel or its congregation. The Reformation was another matter. Henry VIII assumed headship of the Church of England in 1534.

Reformation to Restoration

The monasteries were dissolved between 1536 and 1540. In 1538 royal injunctions were issued governing future church usage; use of the Bible in English, the preaching of sermons, restrictions on the use of candles, removal of saints' images, and so on. This may have been rather a confusing time to the people of Hindon, but may not have seriously inconvenienced them. What happened next threatened the very survival of worship in Hindon, for a time at least.

Henry died in 1547 before his plans to extend the Dissolution to chantry chapels, those private chapels within churches endowed to have masses said for the souls of the worthy departed, could take effect. The nine year old Edward VI succeded. His mentor, Protector Somerset, gave orders for the destruction of all shrines, and a new act was pushed through Parliament to confiscate the assets of all chantries, guilds, 'free chapels' and colleges.

Chantries went. The better endowed Oxford and Cambridge colleges, of course, paid hefty fines and were spared. Hindon was listed as a 'free chapel' and was treated accordingly. The lands supporting the chapel and chaplain were confiscated leaving them presumably without support. In 1549 the Crown sold part of them to Laurence Hyde of London, namely "pasture for 4 oxen yearly in Symerlees (Summerleaze) in tenure of William Deire and lately belonging to late chapel of Hindon." [37] In 1553 commissioners trawled the country removing silver from a vast number of vestries, often leaving only the minimum plate necessary to conduct services. This was a blatant raid to replenish a depleted Exchequer. In Hindon $2\frac{1}{2}$ ounces of silver were taken; a 9 ounce silver chalice was left. Its eventual fate is not known.[38]

The Church in Hindon

Quite what Protestant doctrinal purpose such despoliation might serve is far from clear, but the Crown benefited. The term 'free chapel' seems to refer in this case to Hindon's freedom from the rector's right to appoint its priest (p.23), but other interpretations have been put on the term elsewhere. "Free chapels were exempt from episcopal jurisdiction, and were at first the King's private property," says one.[39] "A free chapel is one which is free or exempt from all ordinary jurisdiction," says another.[40] Neither definition seems to apply here. Hindon, so far as records survive, was clearly subject to visitations, and therefore discipline, by the bishops of Salisbury, and certainly in the 17th century to archdeacons' visitations. East Knoyle vestry records show that archdeacons' visitations were mounted from there, the participants not omitting to charge for expenses. For example, in 1617-18: "Item, for our dinners at the visitation of Hindon, 2.0." (two shillings).

Edward VI died in July 1553 and was shortly succeeded by the Catholic Mary Tudor, who did her best to put the clock back as regards church ritual and the restoration of confiscated endowments. Of course nothing could be done in the case of demolished chapels or lands that had been sold on. Fortunately, most of Hindon's hadn't. The burgesses, in a petition part of which is quoted above (p.23), pleaded that they were "on account of their poverty . . . unable to continue the charges of the chapel and the stipend of the chaplain at their own costs." In October 1558 a royal grant established a chaplain in perpetuity "to celebrate divine service in the said chapel and administer the sacraments from time to time," the living to be called "the free chapel of Hindon in the parish of Est Knoyle." It assigned to the chapel the churchyard, a

Reformation to Restoration

number of tenements in the town with gardens or pasture closes, and two 'shamulas' (shambles) in the market place. (The annual value of this property was £3-7-7d; the value at confiscation had been £3-19-3d). It established a corporation of eight governors, complete with seal, to hold and manage these assets for the chaplain and chapel, and to buy up to a certain limit if they wished, further land for the same purpose, all these grants "without fine or fee."[41] Thereafter the advowson (right of appointment to the living) lay with the Crown.

This emergence of the term 'free chapel' instead of 'chapel-of-ease' seems to have suggested to a number of people that a new building was put up at this point. The idea features largely in *The History of Hindon* by Norah Sheard, 1979, and it has bobbed up from time to time in newspapers and trade directories going back to the 19th century. But both phrases apply to Hindon. 'Chapel-of-ease' is essentially a geographical description of a chapel built some distance from the parish church for the ease of the locals. 'Free chapel' describes its ecclesiastical status. Certainly, in extensive research for this account, no evidence has been seen for any rebuilding at this time, and the idea of a 'Tudor church' must be discarded until and if there is.

Mary died a month after the grant to Hindon chapel. Her motives, if she had been personally involved in the matter apart from merely signing a parchment, would have been to enable the small community to resume its Catholic course. Instead, Protestantism was restored under Elizabeth I. The settlement by Parliament of a Protestant Church of England gradually took shape. The 1559 Act of Uniformity established Elizabeth as supreme governor of the Church of England; a prayer book in English was ordered to be universally used; bishops had to take an oath of loyalty to the monarch (Marian episcopal appointees departed), and all were required to attend worship every Sunday and take the sacrament three times a year, on pain of a shilling fine. We do not know how all this affected Hindon but in 1559 and 1570 presentation to the rectorship of East Knoyle was not by a bishop of Winchester, following the removal of its Marian Bishop White.[42] The early years of James I also saw, in 1604, canons consolidating Elizabethan acts in the regulation of clerical behaviour, the imposition of the 39 Articles, and instructions about church procedures.

All these swings of fortune between Catholicism and Protestantism, with changes of arrangement in churches, and sackings and reappearances of clergy, must have been baffling times to the burgesses, artisans and labourers of Hindon and East Knoyle. In Wiltshire generally there seems to have been little overt complaint, and the country people appear to have kept their heads down, and to have been Protestants under Edward, Catholics under Mary and, for sure, Protestants under Elizabeth.

Hardline Elizabethan measures were, of course, mainly an attempt to stamp out Catholicism, seen as a subversive threat in the years surrounding Catholic Spain's Armada of 1588. But they were also influenced by a lurking threat in the Church of England's ranks, the rapid rise in Elizabeth's last years of sectarianism (nonconformity), and in particular puritanism. One of the issues which puritans used to try to attack the Church of England was that of clerical poverty, and consequent ineffectiveness, that was and had been in countless parishes a disgrace for centuries. Archbishop Whitgift had discovered in 1585 that out of 9000 benefices, over half had incomes of under £10, and most of those under £8. Most clergy had no university degree and 1000 were pluralists (served more than one church). Under half were licensed to preach.

Some of these issues may have surfaced in a violent event in Hindon in 1636, at first sight comic, but which on closer examination may seem to have had its tragic consequences. Samuel Yerworth, or Yearworth had been for nine years curate of Hindon. He must be one of the few clerics who have sought sanctuary in his own church. The details are not all clear in the few surviving legal documents. He had, for reasons obscure, advised a parishioner to leave his wife and child without making provision for their welfare. Quarter Sessions issued a writ to bind Yerworth over, but he fled to the chapel and successfully claimed sanctuary. The constables camped outside in the churchyard and "prevented his egress for a whole day and night until at 3.0 pm (sic) he slipped into his house in the churchyard." The constables then broke down his door and dragged him out, but he somehow got away and made his way to London. There he obtained letters requiring the constables' appearance in the Court of High Commission, an ecclesiastical equivalent of the Court of Star Chamber. This dealt with matters of heresy or schism, crimes committed on holy ground, acts disturbing church services, and sexual offences committed by clerics.

The case seems to have baffled the court and Yerworth's case was dismissed, but the incident has several points of interest. First, it is the earliest mention of the parsonage house in the churchyard, surely the small rectangular building shown in Buckler's drawing of 1804 (p.38). Second, Yerworth mentions in his petition to the court that he had earlier, because of his "extreme poverty", obtained from the Court of Chancery an increase in his stipend from £9 to £16 per annum, with an understanding that it would be increased to £24 on the next renewal of leases of the chapel lands, but that the governors of the trust and tenants had ever since tried to eject him before the leases' renewal. Third, he claimed that he "had ever been a man conformable."[43]

The last phrase may mean that he had conformed to the canons of 1604, in other words was a staunch Church of England man. Could it be that there was an extreme puritan element among the trust governors and tenants that had cobbled together reasons to have him removed? We do not know, but parish registers show that in 1636 he had already been replaced by one George Jenkins, who was still chaplain in 1650 if not beyond, and so not unacceptable to the Commonwealth authorities.

The final oddity in this strange affair is that, although the local constables respected Yerworth's claim of sanctuary, it was in fact invalid, the right having been confined to seven towns in England over a century before.

The Civil War does not seem to have affected Hindon directly, but Edmund Ludlow, future regicide, a native of these parts, manoeuvred his troops near Hindon in the course of his approach to the siege of Wardour Castle in 1643. The rector of East Knoyle, Dr. Christopher Wren, father of the architect, was in 1646 'sequestrated,' or deprived of his living, and fined for alleged

Reformation to Restoration

heresy, for fitting elaborate plasterwork that he had designed into his chancel; this was alleged to be papist representation. The charge was clearly politically motivated. His successor William Clifford, a firm nonconformist, did nothing to remove the work, parts of which may be admired today. (His son, Samuel Clifford, followed him as rector, and was in his turn ejected at the Restoration of the monarchy in 1660).

Despite this, and the damage done to church furnishings by iconoclastic puritans, there is no doubt that under puritan influence a genuine effort was made during the Commonwealth and Protectorate to tackle the problem of plurality and parsonical poverty, and to provide proper stipends which might attract clergy of better education who could preach a decent sermon, a prerequisite of good puritan practice. A Parliamentary survey of parishes in 1649-50 showed how necessary this was in Wiltshire. In Hindon's case, commissioners reported that the curate, George Jenkins, was now receiving a stipend of £24 (the sum poor Yerworth never got), and also temporarily took the tithe of £25, previously paid to the rector in East Knoyle. They recommended, no doubt on petition from the inhabitants, that "it is thought fit and convenient that the Chappell of Hindon belonging to the Church of Knoile bee made a Parish Church of itselfe for the congregation in Hindon."[44] This, however, did not get done.

After the Restoration of the monarchy in 1660, parish churches would have seen a gradual return to Anglican worship. Ecclesiastical courts were restored. The 1662 Act of Uniformity redefined Anglican membership and introduced a revised prayer book. If we could visit Hindon chapel at this time we might notice certain changes from our imaginary medieval visit. Maybe no change to the basic structure, but probably bench seating, with men occupying one side of the church, women the other. There might have been some alteration in the position of the altar or Communion table since puritan days. (Indeed, in the 16th and 17th centuries, its movement must have happened with some regularity. Out into the body of the church as the Lord's Table in times of puritan dominance; back to the east wall as the Altar in high church times). As in the middle ages, Holy Communion would probably not be celebrated more than three or four times a year at high festivals, but two services at least on Sundays, with sermon, would be held. We would also note considerable dilapidation and deficiency, as reported by Hindon chapel wardens at a presentment in Salisbury in 1662:

> ". . . we present the want of the Two Books of Homilies and Bishop Jewell's Apology.
> Item we present the want of a carpitt for the Communion Table.
> . . . Item we present the want of a Surpliss.
> Item . . . we present the want of a Parish Clerke.
> Item . . . we present the want of a Table for Degree of Marriage" (ie Table of Kindred and Affinity).[45]

*Plate 1
Effigy of Bishop Peter des Roches, Winchester Cathedral.
(By kind permission of the Dean & Chapter)*

Plate 2. Hindon old chapel in 1804, as painted by John Buckler. By kind permission of © Devizes Museum (WANHS)

Plate 3. Hindon old chapel in the 19th century, from an original photo in Hindon village archives.

Plate 4. Interior of Hindon Church before 1950, showing former rood screen. Photo, Rawlings & Son Ltd., Hindon.

Plate 5. Hindon Town Band, about 1920. Alban Lamb with baton. Photo, Hindon village archives.

Plate 6. Former Congregational Chapel, Hindon, in 1976.
© *Crown Copyright, NMR.*

Plate 7. Former Primitive Methodist Chapel, Hindon, in 1998.
Photo, R. Dewhurst.

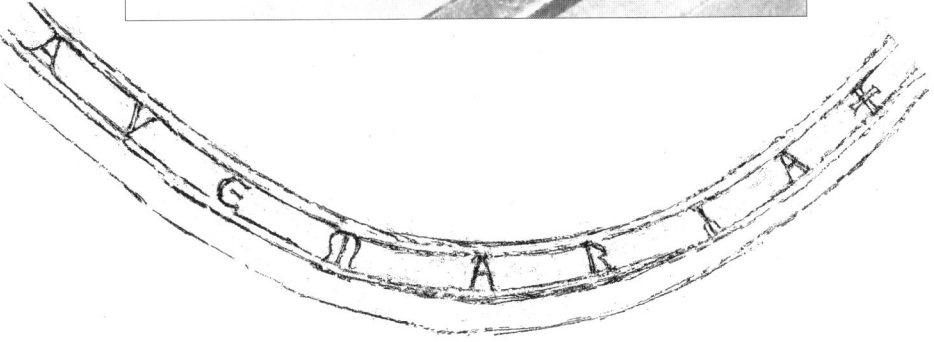

*Plate 8. The Pertwood Bell and rubbing of inscription.
Photo, R. Dewhurst.*

*Left: Plate 9.
Imprint of seal of
Governors of the Free
Chapel of Hindon, 1779.*

*Below: Plate 10.
Clock mechanism,
Hindon Church.
Photo, R. Dewhurst.*

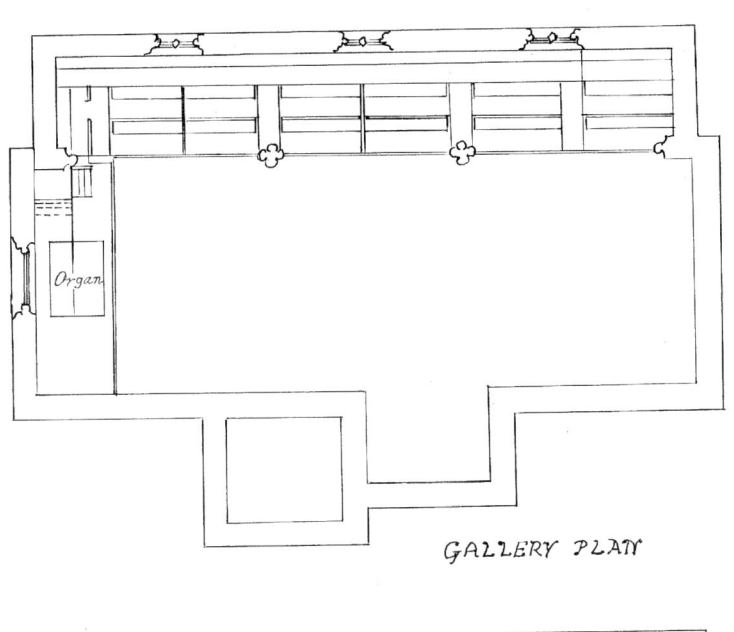

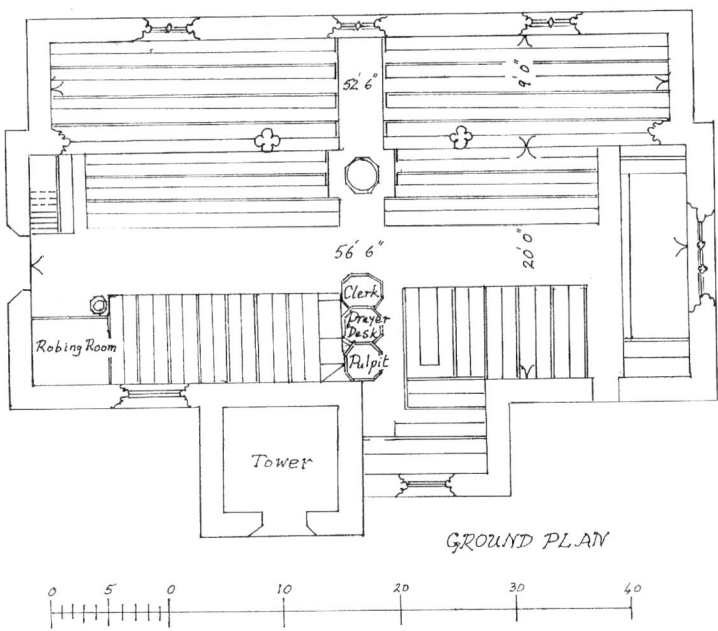

Plate 11. Hindon old chapel in 1869, drawn by T.H. Wyatt. From plans in Wilts & Swindon Record Office, Trowbridge.

WEST ELEVATION

EAST ELEVATION

Plate 12. Hindon old chapel in 1869, drawn by T.H. Wyatt. From plans in Wilts & Swindon Record Office, Trowbridge.

The 18th Century

What of the condition of surviving Catholics in the area at this time and into the 18th century? Laws passed from Elizabeth onward prevented them entering Parliament, holding any public office, upholding the Pope's authority, or celebrating Mass, at least openly. This is unlikely to have affected the few Catholics in Hindon much, but the laws against recusancy (absence from the services and sacraments of the Church of England) did, and a succession of acts increased the penalties involved. As time went on and suspicion against Catholics diminished, these laws served a cautionary purpose rather than being automatically applied, and JPs, who had to enforce anti-recusancy laws, were often relaxed or even absent-minded in their application.

This was as well for the Catholics, for south west Wiltshire was an important focus for Catholic recusants, centred on two families, the Arundells of Wardour and the Stourtons of Stourton, on whose estates services were discreetly held. Hindon contributed a few to the congregation at Wardour in the 18th century, but not to the extent of Tisbury, which had the largest recorded number of any Wiltshire parish. Sources are sparse and sometimes contradictory, but it seems that Hindon Catholics were always in single figures between 1661 and 1783, with a top count of seven in four of those years. They included a glover, a baker, a brazier and a 'barber chyrurgion' called Robert White, in the late 17th century and another surgeon, Henry Lambert, in the 18th. Philip Kelloway, innkeeper, made numerous appearances at Quarter Sessions for recusancy, and was probably fined, but he carried on his trade. Lambert, when listed by the incumbent in 1767, had already lived quietly in Hindon for

The Church in Hindon

thirty years, and was probably still around in 1783, by which time the number of Catholics in Hindon had fallen to three.[46]

Lambert's name brings us neatly back to the Anglican story, for it is probably he who is listed in replies to a questionnaire sent to all Wiltshire parishes in Bishop Barrington's inaugural visitation in 1783. The replies from John Evans, Hindon curate, give quite a vivid picture of the chapel and its congregation at that time:

"1. Divine service is performed (on Sunday) at half past eleven o'clock in the morning, and at half past three in afternoon. Prayers and preaching in the morning. Prayers in the afternoon.

2. There are prayers every Wednesday and Friday throughout the year.

3. (I serve) as curate.

4. I serve the church of Pertwood once a fortnight, a mile from Hindon. In the intermediate space I serve Teffont Evias in the morning. I have no licence to this cure.

5. The sacrament is regularly administered, at Christmas, Easter, Whitsun and Michaelmas.

6. There are in general about 20 communicants . . .

7. There is one family of reputed papists consisting of three persons, the master of which is a surgeon and apothecary. They have no public place of worship in this parish, nor is any popish priest resident in it, neither any popish school kept.

8. There are no Presbyterians, Independants, Anabaptists or Quakers in this parish.

The 18th century

9. The children and servants (of parishioners) are catechized in Lent and at other convenient times.

10. There is a register regularly kept of births and burials, in good preservation.

11. It has not been usual to marry in Hindon, the parishioners of which always are married at Knoyle.

12. This is a chapel of ease to East Knoyle.

13. There is no terrier (register of church property and goods) belonging to this chapel to be found at Hindon, it being tithable to East Knoyle.

14. There is a free school endowed by William Beckford Esq. The master's name is Thomas Ransom.

15. (no reply given to question about church wardens).

16. There is no school but what is mentioned in the 14th article. It is supported by Mr. Beckford's contribution alone for boys and girls. They are instructed in the Christian religion.

17. I reside the major part of my time in Hindon, but not in the parsonage house.

18. The minister distributes the money given at the offertory to the poor communicants.

19. (My place of residence is) partly at Hindon and partly at Fovant. The former the nearest post town."[47]

It is commonplace to view the not very religious 18th century as a time of church decay and neglect. In terms of church fabric, this was often true. However the editor of the above return comments that, by the not very exacting standards of the day, the Wiltshire clergy on the whole performed their duties fairly well. Clearly here pluralism was still present. John Evans had a heavy workload. His brother was a curate at Teffont Evias and clearly needed his assistance.

Four years before, the management of the charity founded by the royal patent of 1558 (p.26) had fallen into chaos through death and failure to appoint new governors. Forty citizens petitioned George III, pleading that the chapel was "likely to run into utter decay" and the proceeds of the land likely to be diverted to other purposes. Letters Patent of 24 March 1779 appointed new governors and re-established the grant with very similar conditions.[48] This is the earliest document so far seen that refers to the chapel by its present dedication to St. John, Baptist, but it is likely that this goes back earlier, possibly to the Restoration of 1660. A new seal was also issued at this time (plate 9).

Evans' reply to Q. 17 of the 1783 questionnaire suggests that the parsonage house, presumably Yerworth's former abode, was either derelict or too small for him. He says nothing about money, but we know from other sources that Hindon's curate was still wretchedly poor, and the endowment of the chapel inadequate. If the reader can bear a few figures, this is best illustrated by comparisons. At the confiscation of the chapel lands in about 1547 the living had been worth £3-19-3d. A few years earlier the rectory of the much smaller Chicklade had been worth £11-5-0d, while 253 years earlier East Knoyle had been worth £40! At the 1649-50 Parliamentary survey (p.31) Hindon, with a temporary reversion to its chaplain of its tithes from East Knoyle, was worth £49; East Knoyle was worth £230 and Downton £400. The tale continued.

Even much later, an averaging of values over the years 1829-31 gives East Knoyle (population 1028) a figure of £850; Sutton Veney (pop. 848), £800; and Hindon (pop. 921), £75. Tiny Pertwood (pop. 29), with its very own rector, was six years later worth £74.[49]

This is the world reported on by William Cobbett, recording in *Rural Rides* his journey in 1826 up the lush and beautiful Nadder valley in September, and possibly through Hindon, though he does not mention the town. On the old curmudgeon goes on his horse northwards, spluttering with indignation that out of 24 parishes between Heytesbury and Warminster, two parsonage houses have disappeared and another five are uninhabitable because the incumbents could not afford to maintain them.

Towards a new parish and church

For some of these poor Wiltshire clergy, isolated in downland villages, educated somewhat above most of their parishioners, life must have been extremely lonely if they were not on good communication routes and could not easily visit each other. Hindon, on major coaching routes, would have been a better place than some, and from this time some things began gradually to improve. In 1821 the endowment was augmented by a one-off payment of £400 from Queen Anne's Bounty, a fund for the relief of poor parishes drawn from ecclesiastical revenues confiscated by Henry VIII and donations from richer clergy. This sum was invested in three per cent Consols, dividends being paid to the chaplain.[50] In 1844 the Tithe Commissioners awarded a rent charge or money payment of £70 pa in lieu of tithe of corn etc. to the Rector of East Knoyle;[51] in fact it is likely that the money payments

The Church in Hindon

had begun some time before. However, it seems that Rectors allowed the chaplains of Hindon to receive at least the great tithe from this date. In 1848 celebration of marriages in the chapel was authorized, and the fees collected.[52] In 1868 the Charity Commission ordered the sale of all church property in Hindon, and the resultant £3000 was invested instead. Finally, in 1869, Hindon was separated from East Knoyle parish, became a district chapelry, and the living a vicarage. William Milles was appointed vicar and within two years, with what must have seemed to him almost miraculous speed, he had a brand new church.

From the beginning of the 19th century we at last get some idea of the appearance of the old chapel that was pulled down for the new church. Sir Richard Colt Hoare of Stourhead (1758-1838), historian and antiquarian of Wiltshire, commissioned the watercolour artist John Buckler (1770-1851) to paint hundreds of Wiltshire churches, a beautiful and comprehensive collection preserved in the museum in Devizes. He painted Hindon Chapel in 1804 (plate 2); its structure is discussed in the separate section below (p.49).

We do not know what repairs or alterations had been done before 1804, but in 1808 letters patent required East Knoyle to make public collection to "take down, enlarge and rebuild the Chapel of Hindon." This shows that East Knoyle had some responsibility for its upkeep. The target was £1886-15-8d, a considerable sum.[53] The appeal only raised a fraction of that, and new letters patent were issued in 1813. Other records of this appeal are confusing, and it is not clear how much was collected or what repairs were made,[54] except that, as shown by charity documents, the chapel was in 1814 re-pewed at the expense of certain parishioners who reserved 10 pews for their own use, the rest being free to all. Other work may have been extensive, for two gazeteers of the 1830s describe the chapel as "modern".

In 1836 the chapel was altered and extended by William Gover (c. 1814-1859), a surveyor and architect from Winchester, or possibly by his father of the same name.[55] These works cannot have been very solid, for in 1869 part of the roof fell in and the chapel was stated to be "totally unfit for the performance of Divine Service."[56] Architects recommended a total rebuild that resulted in the church that we see today.

The estimated cost was £3,100, which was guaranteed in full by Richard Grosvenor, second Marquis of Westminster (1795-1869), who then owned a substantial portion of the village. His chosen architect was Thomas Henry Wyatt (1807-1880), not to be confused with James Wyatt "the destroyer", who demolished much medieval work at Salisbury Cathedral and erected Fonthill Abbey. Thomas Wyatt was a major player in Wiltshire in what can only be described as the mid-Victorian obsession with tinkering with parish churches. According to Pevsner[57] he repaired, altered or replaced sixty churches in Wiltshire alone.

In Hindon the old chapel was taken down, together with a shop to the north of the present Post Office, and probably the remains of the old parsonage seen in Buckler's picture, last let in 1831. The new church was built on the same site, re-using some stone, the six bells, the clockface and memorial tablets from the old. While work was in progress, services were held in the National Schoolroom, now the present school in School Lane.[58]

The Church in Hindon

Westminster did not live to see the church built, and the Dowager Marchioness wrote the cheque. The building was consecrated on 6 July 1871 by Bishop Moberly. "About two o'clock the Bishop and clergy and a number of ladies and gentlemen partook of an excellent cold luncheon at the National Schoolroom, which was well provided by Mr. Hacker of the Lamb Inn, and gave great satisfaction. The Hindon Band played during the evening and did themselves much credit."[59]

Why was a new church built? Decay of the old, if true, is an obvious first reason. The generosity of the wealthier clergy and even more so the enlightened landowners in this period clearly provided such opportunities. Need for more seating was not an issue. The new church is 40 feet longer than the old, yet was designed to seat only 376, as opposed to 360 formerly, this in a time of gently declining population (771 in 1841, 603 in 1871). The internal design of the present church as opposed to the old chapel (p.50) followed a trend in early Victorian times that was to some extent influenced by the High Church movement (also called the Oxford Movement, or tractarianism) in attempting to revert to pre-puritan arrangements. Galleries and box pews went. Some rood screens were restored. Medieval-style pulpits and lecterns were firmly placed at the east end of naves, replacing elaborate 17th century fittings in other positions. Surpliced choirs sat in chancels between the congregation and the altar, which was usually at the extreme east end. This general plan was followed here, and it may be that there would not have been room for it in the old building. There used to be a rood screen that was removed probably in the late 1940s or in 1950. It is said to have been of the same

Towards a new parish and church

wood as the pews, and so probably also dated from the 1870-1 rebuild (plate 4).

There are precious few surviving records of how matters were conducted in the 19th century; certainly nothing to suggest that practice in Hindon has been any other than middle-of-the-road Anglican. There is no book recording services, but bishops' visitation records show a gradual increase in the frequency of sacramental services since the medieval and early modern periods. In 1864 there were two 'full' services every Sunday, at 10.30 am and 6 pm, Holy Communion twice a month and at Easter, either Whit or Trinity Sunday, and sometimes at Christmas.[60] In 1876 Communion was celebrated at 8 am every Sunday except the first in the month, and at Christmas, Easter, Ascension, Whit and Trinity Sundays, together with the normal morning and evening services with sermon. There survive brief notes taken from an apparently lost vestry minute book covering the years 1832-1920. These reflect a fairly placid conduct of the sort of affairs that vestries used to cover: raising of church rates, appointment of annual chapel wardens, appointment of overseers of the poor and waywardens, and so on. In the winter months many vestry meetings were adjourned from the chapel or church to the warmth of the Lamb, the Grosvenor Arms, the Swan or the Queen's Head. Attendance could be poor. An all-time low was achieved on 26 April 1886, when only the vicar and two churchwardens were present. An unanimous vote of thanks to the churchwardens was passed. For turning up? Democracy can get no more direct than this.

One aspect of services that should be commemorated is that of the famous Hindon Town Band, already noted as active at the consecration ceremony of the new church. They played in church too, and the *S. Wilts Church Magazine* of May 1907 recorded that at Easter "the organ was assisted (as on every first Sunday in the month) by a cornet, two violins, and a piccolo, and the singing was very congregational." Balance must have been a problem, though. One wonders whether this tradition in Hindon may have gone back to pre-organ days (viz. Hardy's *Under the Greenwood Tree*). A fantasy, perhaps. The last recorded performance in church of this band, refounded after the First World War, was at the Harvest Festival in September 1930, when having tootled in the Square under the leadership of J. Snook, they accompanied "some" of the hymns in church (plate 5).

Nonconformism

Protestant sects had found fertile soil in Wiltshire from an early date, and martyrs are recorded from the early 16th century. William Clifford, the rector of East Knoyle already mentioned (p.31), was one of a commission set up in 1654 to eject scandalous and negligent Anglican clergy. The sectarians were dominant during the Civil War, the Commonwealth and the Protectorate, but from the 1660 restoration of the monarchy, when all clergy were required to conform to the Book of Common Prayer or be expelled, nonconformists began for the first time not to be acceptable at Anglican services, and this led to dissenting groups setting up their own arrangements. From 1689, nonconformists could license their meeting houses for public worship at quarter sessions, and the 18th century saw a rapid increase in such registrations.

Two churches, Congregational and Primitive Methodist, were

Nonconformism

to make a strong impact on Hindon. Both were regarded by many mainstream Anglicans of the time as being vaguely subversive, and they seem in consequence to have kept few records, at any rate in early days. Much of the following is therefore derived from folk memory or subsequent oral inquiry.

The Congregationalists were successors to a puritan sect, then usually called Independents, that had played a major role during the Civil War and Interregnum. Similar in doctrine to Presbyterians, they believed in considerable freedom of thought and action for individual congregations. A remarkable woman, Mrs. Joanna Turner, had in the mid 18th century attended dissenting chapels in Bristol and Trowbridge, and encouraged the establishment of local groups for weekday worship, moving to Tisbury in 1781. She extended her influence to Hindon. In about 1810 a philanthropic Warminster minister built a chapel seating about 100 in the east Dene, perhaps intentionally on land then just outside the parish boundary (plate 6). It was said that this activity provoked much hostility from the villagers, and that men on horseback had to be deployed to hold off hostile attacks during building. The chapel received intermittent financial aid from outside Congregational organisations, but it may be that continuity of ministers, and therefore of worship, was a problem. From 1854 the congregation had links with a new chapel in East Knoyle, whose members were successors to those served by that Samuel Clifford who had been ejected from the East Knoyle rectorship at the Restoration (p.31). This association lasted for over a century, except for 1961-3, when Hindon linked up with the chapel in Tisbury. Membership later declined; the chapel was sold in 1972, and in 1999 was a private house called The Old Chapel.[61]

The second movement, the Primitive Methodists, otherwise known as 'Ranters', were a breakaway from the mainstream, Wesleyan Methodists from 1812. They were humble people, mainly urban poor and farm labourers, and by the 1870s were associated with agricultural trade unionism. There was plenty here to excite the hostility of mainstream Hindonians, and their efforts to build a chapel were obstructed even more than those of the Congregationalists. In 1840 they obtained title to a plot to the west of the upper High Street just off Back Way, probably on land now belonging to the property called Quoins. This was then in open fields with, probably, lane access from the High Street. The farmer occupying the surrounding land locked the gate, and the faithful were driven to manhandling building stones over a stile to the site before daylight and after dark, even the women carrying loads in their aprons. Worship continued here for many years with, at one time, a congregation of 90 and a Sunday School of 70. In 1877 alterations were made at the expense of the mainly poor members, box pews being removed and a porch added. In 1898, village hostility presumably having abated, a new chapel was built in the lower High Street. After the reunion of the various Methodist churches in 1932 the 'Primitive' appellation was dropped. There was a schoolroom behind the chapel that during the Second World War served as a canteen for the forces encamped in the area. The chapel closed in April 1981; at the time of writing it is a craft shop, also called The Old Chapel (plate 7).[62]

Hindon church in modern times

To return to the Church of England, in 1885 a grant of stipend by the Ecclesiastical Commissioners to Hindon's vicar was issued,[63] one step in the Church's slow movement from a land-based to a salaried system of supporting its clergy. This gave the incumbent the yearly sum of ten pounds. A nationwide survey of 1893 focused attention on the inequality of the value of benefices, the first concerted study since the Commonwealth. A Clergy Relief Fund was set up, but it was to be the 20th century that was to see a very slow phasing-out of the remains of the tithe system, and an equalization of clerical stipends.

At the end of the First World War Hindon was temporarily without its vicar, Marshall Lumsden, who was seconded as chaplain to the armed forces for 18 months prior to April 1919. Even without such emergencies the old problem of shortage of clergy, leading to pluralism, remained, and was partly to be tackled by the merging of parishes and alteration of some boundaries. This brought Chicklade and Pertwood into the orbit of Hindon.

All Saints was an 1832 rebuild of a 12th century church in Chicklade, a small village and parish straddling the present A303, two miles to the north. From 1899, when its population was about 60, its rector also held St. Peter's Pertwood, an even smaller place whose highest ever census population figure was 38, in 1881. Pertwood's small 14th century church was completely rebuilt in the 19th century, retaining a few medieval fittings. Because it had been a small manor in Saxon times, it earned an entry in Domesday (which Hindon, of course, did not). Its former rectors often lived in Hindon, there being so few buildings in Pertwood. In 1922 the

The Church in Hindon

two parishes of Chicklade and Pertwood were amalgamated, and the resultant parish joined with that of Hindon under one vicar, the two elements remaining separate. If that is confusing, it was simplified fifty years later when the junction was completed, and in 1972 the parish became that of 'Hindon with Chicklade and Pertwood.'[64]

All Saints Chicklade escaped closure, and services are still held there, usually two or three times a month. St. Peter's, however, had become derelict, and in 1968 had been closed. The only bell, probably cast in Salisbury in the late 13th century, was taken to Hindon church for safe keeping. The bell is the ninth oldest and the oldest inscribed Wiltshire bell. Its Catholic inscription "+ AVE : MARIA" probably escaped the attention of destructively minded 17th century puritans because the bell was such a tight fit in St. Peter's belfry that only an acrobat could have read the text. It remains the property of Hindon Parochial Church Council (PCC), but was transferred to the present Salisbury and South Wilts. Museum in Salisbury on loan in 1973, where it may be seen as part of a display of historic Wiltshire bells (plate 8).

St. Peter's was declared redundant in January 1972 and sold to the then owners of Manor Farm, formerly Pertwood Manor. In recent years it has been handsomely restored by its later owners, Mr. and Mrs. J. Giles. Various internal fittings that had been dispersed were replaced, and in 1998 a specially cast replica of the old bell was hung in the belfry, restoring to the surrounding countryside a sound familiar over so many centuries. A service is held in the church at least once a year.

The amalgamation of these parishes was not the only change.

Hindon church in modern times

The 1970s and 1980s were a period of much experimentation in and reorganisation of pastoral care in the diocese. Deaneries were reordered in 1973 and 1975, the latter year seeing Hindon removed from the dissolved Shaftesbury and Tisbury Deanery and returned to Chalke, to which it had belonged throughout historical times. As to parishes, several proposed rearrangements were floated, and some of them tried, most of which seem to have resulted in one parish losing its right to a vicarage. Hindon, for example, was reunited with East Knoyle as a benefice between 1975 and 1986, when the latter lost this right. In 1988 a number of further adjustments resulted in the completion of the Tisbury Anglican Team Ministry, which had been in formation for some time. It now comprises the parishes of

Tisbury
Swallowcliffe
Ansty
Chilmark
Hindon with Chicklade and Pertwood
Fonthill Bishop with Berwick St. Leonard
Fonthill Gifford

In preparation for this fusion Hindon with Chicklade and Pertwood had ceased to be a benefice in 1985 and the patron's right of appointment was then applied to presentation to the Team Rectorship. Presentation was to be exercised by the Lord Chancellor "in right of the Crown" one turn in four; on the remaining occasions by the Diocesan Board of Patronage. The Rector then became responsible, with the Bishop, for appointing a Team Vicar, who presently cares for Hindon.

The Church in Hindon

As to the services in Hindon church, we know that, from 1935 there was generally a Sunday regime familiar to older generations of churchgoers and based on the Book of Common Prayer: Communion at 8 am, Matins or 'Morning Prayer' at 10.30 or 11.00, and Evensong or 'Evening Prayer' at 6 pm. Different clergy introduced different minor modifications to the main Sunday morning service, Communion directly following Matins or replacing it once a month, 'Family Communion' sometimes appearing in place of Matins or Evensong, and so on. From the late 1980s the number of sacramental services began to increase further. At the time of writing Parish Communion is the main Sunday morning service, with Matins taking place only once a month.

HINDON OLD CHAPEL
– A DESCRIPTON

The Buckler picture of 1804 (p.38, plate 2) shows a simple structure in which nave and chancel seem to form one unit; an early medieval tower with entry through a pointed arched doorway to the south and considerable patching on its west side. VCH/Wilts describes the west door and window, and the window in the small south transept as later medieval. We know from an annotation on the parish register of 1680 that there were doors on the north side set with two small seats.

The *Bath Journal* reported that Hindon's Great Fire of 1754 "did some small damage to the Church".

Colt Hoare in 1822 described the chapel as "a plain turreted building... its length is 57 feet; its breadth 19 feet 3 inches. It was repaired in 1814; it is neatly pewed, but much injured in its effect by a large gallery built over the lower range of pews. The east and west windows are enlivened by some squares of modern painted glass... The font is octagon, but not ancient." What he calls the "lower range of pews" were probably those on the north.[65]

Manuscript notes by a Sir Stephen Glynne, who visited the chapel in June 1849 after Gover's reconstruction of 1836 (p.39) remark:

The Church in Hindon

"This Church is completely modernised and scarcely deserving any notice. It has a body, north aisle, south transept, and a small tower on the south. The latter is original – having plain parapet and string, two stages of double lancet windows, and no buttresses. It may perhaps be of debased work. The west door is pointed with the hood and fair mouldings. All the rest is wretched . . . (illeg.) work."[66]

Two photographs taken not long before the old chapel was demolished show it much infested with ivy, and with a round-headed window on the south, west of the tower, replacing Buckler's double lancet window (plate 3). This was presumably a result of Gover's reconstruction. An octagonal clockface has replaced Buckler's small diamond-shaped one. This was later transferred to the new church, though the present clock mechanism is later (p.56, plate 10).

Wyatt's specification for the new church required re-use of as much of the old chapel's external dressed stone facings as possible, "made up with Chilmark stone."[67] It therefore seems likely that the chapel was faced with Chilmark, as indeed it seems to be in Buckler's drawing.

Wyatt made drawings of the old chapel before it was pulled down; they give us a comprehensive picture of it in its last days (plates 11 & 12). They show Gover's new north aisle as a rather awkwardly tacked-on flat-roof extension housing, inside, pews running east-west on the ground floor and in a gallery that must have cut across the windows on the north side. The organ sat in a southward extension of this gallery at the west end, and must have

Hindon old chapel

blocked light from the west window. Alf Lamb, an old inhabitant of the village said of this instrument many years ago that it was a "handle-turned affair."[68] It is not clear what this meant, unless it was a barrel organ or a combined barrel and finger organ, which would have been blown by means of a rotating handle which simultaneously turned the mechanism.

On the ground floor entry seems to have been through the tower arch, then right and left past pulpit, prayer desk and clerk's seat to the middle aisle. Pews on the south side were mostly at right angles to the middle aisle. The impression on a preacher in the pulpit would be not unlike that on an actor on an apron stage or on an oratorio conductor with his musicians about him and the chorus facing him in the gallery. With the chapel full, it would have seemed very intimate, and close.

The chapel seated 360, of which 210 places were "free and unappropriated," that is, not rented by the gentry. The pews appear from the plan to be open; there is no information as to whether or not they had been boxed at an earlier date.

Colt Hoare records two memorial floor tablets that were not transferred to the new church, and cannot be identified in the churchyard. They commemorated:

George Hancock, Sept. 16 1758, aged 38.
Mrs. Ann Money, wife of Richard Money, 15 Jan. 1793, aged 30.
Rev. William Rees, Curate of Hindon, 13 Feb. 1805, aged 52.

THE CHURCH OF ST. JOHN THE BAPTIST, HINDON

Wyatt's church of 1870/71, a Grade II listed building, stands as we have seen on the site of the old chapel, possibly on a marginally differing alignment, and set back slightly further from the street. Its overall length is 91 feet, as opposed to 57 feet for its predecessor; the width across nave and aisles is 45 feet 4 inches. The spire is believed to be just over 100 feet high. It is said that the foundations were sunk 3 feet lower than before. The architect's specification foresaw some disturbance of old graves during the building, and folk memory has it that this indeed occurred. There is no known record that Hindon's burial ground was ever anywhere else but here.

Exterior

Wyatt's design was in what the Victorians understood to be Early English style. The basic elevation, although it is much more elaborate, pays some compliment to that of the old chapel in keeping the general arrangement of entry through its (3-stage) tower on the south side. The rather pleasing cluster of windows in two gables to the lean-to roof of the south aisle echo to some extent the old chapel's mini-transept on the south next to the tower. The three gabled sets of windows to the north aisle are a much better

The Church of St. John the Baptist

arrangement than the extraordinary flat-roofed north extension on Gover's 1836 alterations.

We have seen (p.50) that the architect specified Chilmark stone for the external facing; he also ordered dressings of Red Bed Farleigh Down stone. With variable weathering, it is not easy to follow the distinction between them. Weathering of the (presumed) Chilmark stone on the spire has given it the unfortunate appearance of concrete. The low rake of the rooves, with comparatively small windows below is a characteristic Wyatt feature that can be seen in more extreme form at All Saints, Chitterne.

The panel over the west door shows the Agnus Dei, emblem of Christ the Lamb of God rather than of John the Baptist, who is normally shown in church representations in desert garb and pointing to the Lamb. But he also often carries a book showing the Agnus Dei, and in medieval times was thought, by association, to protect all those involved in the wool trade. This may possibly relate to the current dedication of the church.[69]

In the churchyard, the grave of the first vicar, Milles, is to be found near the south east corner of the chancel. The chest tomb of Joseph Hacker, d. 1844, and his wife Elizabeth lies about 6 yards east of the chancel and is Grade II listed. The three beautifully incised gravestones to the north of it are worth noting. There are two First World War headstones, erected by the Commonwealth War Graves Commission, to A. F. Stevens and C. K. Ingram. Interestingly, that to Stevens indicates that his trade in the Machine Gun Corps was "shoeing smith". Finally, a stone to the north of the church commemorates D. L. Small, killed on a live-firing exercise in 1943.

The Church in Hindon

The war memorial by the west door stood at the road crossing in the Square when dedicated in 1919. At that time it was surmounted by a stone lantern and looked better proportioned. It was moved to its present position after being demolished by a runaway tank of the Irish Guards in 1943. The lantern was presumably unrestorable.

The Millennium Arch over the churchyard south gates, made by David Tomlin, was designed to echo, as far as possible, the motives on Wyatt's original and surviving gates.

Interior

Inside, as outside, all is of a piece and little altered (although repaired) since the first building. Pulpit, font and Communion rail all appear to be contemporary; there is no trace of what happened to their predecessors in the old chapel. Internal stone dressings are of Corsham Down stone, a yellowish coarse-grained oolitic limestone from a now defunct quarry. It appears also to have been used on external string courses over the west door. The coloured glass in nave, aisles and west end is 'rolled cathedral glass', made by a machine-rolled process that produces a textured surface. It is still made. The provenance of the stained glass in the east windows is not known.

Taking the church anti-clockwise, the photograph to the right of the south door shows the old chapel a few years before demolition.

The organ, by Eustace Ingram of London NW, has two manuals, tracker action of 1884, 11 speaking stops and 4 couplers. It was installed in 1886; an electric blower was added in 1949. Ingram's organs were well made and durable, not noted for inventiveness or tonal sophistication, but perfectly adequate for normal parish church use. This example has been described as particularly fine, with robust clear tone. Virtually unaltered, it is still in excellent order after over 100 years' regular use. It was not completed; there is room for one extra stop on the swell. Wyatt's drawings suggest that it replaced a smaller instrument that stood at the west end of the north aisle. This may have been transferred from the gallery of the old chapel (p.50).

The Lady Chapel, at the east end of the north aisle, was consecrated in 1957. The blue and gold reredos curtain and altar frontal were made from material used in Westminster Abbey at the coronation of Queen Elizabeth II in 1953, and subsequently sold to a number of parish churches. It is made of silk farmed, thrown and woven in England. The design is by Prof. R. Y. Gooden. More may be seen at St. James, Ansty.

The Church Room, at the west end of the north aisle, and most of the adjoining storage and kitchen facilities, date from the formation of the Tisbury Team Ministry in 1988, when Hindon lost its right to a vicarage and a meeting place was needed. The screen dividing it from the body of the church is an elegant feature. A plaque inside commemorates Gemma, Miriam and Delia, daughters of the Revd. Malcolm and Pauline Acheson, who died in a vicarage fire at Chilmark on 15 March 1989, a tragedy that received national media coverage.

The royal arms over the west door are those of William IV. They were painted by G. Snook of Hindon in 1835. The origin of the panel is uncertain; for many years it was stored and hung outside

The Church in Hindon

the village, and has only recently been repatriated. It may have hung over Hindon's former Quarter Sessions, which were once held in the Lamb Inn, and from 1867 to 1889 in what is now the village hall. Its large size, however, suggests that it may have come from the old chapel. An exposition of the heraldry hangs nearby. The charmingly idiosyncratic face of the lion has led to suggestions that this might be a self portrait of Snook.

Of the memorial plaques at the west end the most interesting is that over the south door to James Ames, who died in 1828. "Many years the kind and active surgeon of this town", he "bequeathed a service of sacramental plate to this Chapel and Ten Pounds annually to the Poor." The plate is still in use. The money was originally distributed in bread, and in calico to poor widows. In 1979 there were still Hindonians who could remember going on Christmas Eve to what is now Albany House and receiving loaves from Alban Lamb through a sash window.[70]

The clock, on the second stage of the tower, is by Gillett and Bland of Croydon, 1875. It has an early example of a gravity escapement in the now unusual form of a 'single 14-legged' design (plate 10).

The commissioners of 1553 (p.25) recorded two bells in Hindon chapel. There are now six, all inscribed, at the third stage of the tower, which, as bells should, tell their own story:-

1. Treble. F. 4 cwt. "Peace & good neighbourhood." AR. 1754.
2. E flat. $4\frac{1}{2}$ cwt. "When you us ring we sweetly sing." A. R. 1754.
3. D flat. $5\frac{1}{4}$ cwt. "Prosperity to this Town." A. R. 1754.
4. C. $5\frac{3}{4}$ cwt. "Abel Rudhall [of Gloucester] cast us all." A. R. 1754.

The Church of St. John the Baptist

5. B flat. 7 cwt. "Thomas Feild, Gentn Bailiff." A. R. 1754.
6. Tenor. A flat. 9 cwt. "Five bells cast into six w. additional metal at the expense of William Beckford and Bisse Richard, Esq." A. R. 1754.

Hindon church and its architect have not had a good press. "A reduced, less successful version of his church at Fonthill Gifford" sniffs Pevsner, who gets its building date wrong.[71] Wyatt's work generally has been criticised for rigidity, and his control of his projects as slack. The heaviness of Hindon's spire has engendered much dislike, and the view has even been expressed locally that demolition of the old chapel was an act of vandalism. This may be too extreme. Despite the charm of Buckler's drawing, the former chapel was not of particular architectural merit, was very bare, and probably beyond economical repair. Wyatt's church, near the top of the High Street and at a slight angle to it, dominates superbly, particularly when seen from the bottom of the village, and its spire can be seen from all the hills around. Entering the church gives a feeling of openness and of light, despite Wyatt's low roof rake and in contrast to the gloom of Pevsner's favoured Fonthill Gifford. The choir stalls are cramped and uncomfortable, but the clergy find the sightlines and acoustics good, particularly from the pulpit. The Lady Chapel is a successful area for small services, the church can be made warm, and it provides a flexible space for a variety of purposes. This we owe partly to the much criticised Victorian church re-designers.

APPENDIX A

Chaplains/curates of old Hindon Chapel

1393	William Stok
1622-5	Symon Stephens
1626	Christopher Willan
1627-36	Samuel Yerworth or Yearworth
1638-50	George Jenkins
1668-76	John Moyle
1680	John Ellis
1679-83	Samuell Stone
1710-21	Sam Stone, not necessarily identical with above
1728-30	William Nairn
1730-6	Richard Randall
1774-80	John Nairn
1776	L. Jones
1780-3	John Evans
d. 1805	William Rees
1813-21	William Norris
1821	Henry Boucher, alternating with above
1822-6	W. W. Phelps
1827-9	Christopher Nevill
1829-54	Charles Harbin
1855-66	Robert Graves Walker, 'perpetual curate'
1866-7	Francis Gell
1867-9	William Milles, 'perpetual curate,' becomes vicar 1869

Pre-19th century records are fragmentary, often ill-kept and sometimes contradictory. This list derives mainly from parish registers (starting fitfully in 1599), bishops' transcripts and bishops' registers. Only names seen by the writer and described as 'chaplain' or 'curate', and for the years stated, are included. Some may have served longer.

The Patron was the Crown, at latest from 1558. The right of appointment may have been exercised by the Lord Chancellor "in right of the Crown" from the Reformation.

A 'perpetual curate' was a priest nominated by a lay patron and licensed by the bishop to serve a church without a vicar. He then had a lifelong tenure.

APPENDIX B

Vicars of Hindon

dates of presentation	name	patron
1869	William Milles	Lord Chancellor
1882	William Henry Lewis	Lord Chancellor
1886	Henry Walter Taylor	Lord Chancellor
1897	Julian Pattison	Lord Chancellor
1908	Marshal Winder Lumsden (from 1922 with Chicklade & Pertwood)	Lord Chancellor
1932	Ven. George Henry Hogbin	Viscount Weymouth
1938	Charles Francis Wellesley Wilkinson	Lord Chancellor
1948	Walter Henry Cook	Marquis of Bath
1952	Henry Stephen Fussell	Lord Chancellor
1956	Cecil Anstruther Duke-Baker	Diocesan Board of Patronage
1960	Bruce George Beale, CBE	Lord Chancellor
1967	Charles Kemp Buck	Lord Chancellor
1971	John Gabriel Scott, OBE	Lord Chancellor
1974	Lionel William Daffurn, DFC	Lord Chancellor

dates of presentation	*name*	*patron*
1985	Rt. Revd. Eric Arthur John Mercer (Priest in Charge)	–
1988	James Malcolm Acheson (Team Vicar)	–
1995	Richard Wren (Team Vicar)	–

Daffurn was the last incumbent (holder of freehold to the benefice, or ecclesiastical living) of Hindon. Thereafter patronage (right of appointment, or advowson) was applied to the Rectorship of Tisbury Team Ministry (p.47).

REFERENCES

References are generally to the most accessible version of the information. For example, the *Victoria County History / Wilts* is available in the larger public libraries locally, and contains its own index to anterior sources.

1 Gazeteer of prehistoric traces in *Victoria County History/Wilts (VCH/Wilts)* i.
2 *Ancient Trackways of Wessex*, Timperley & Brill, Phoenix House, 1965.
3 *The Place-Names of Wiltshire*, Gover, Mawer & Stenton, English Place-Name Society, xvi, CUP 1939. *English Place-Name Elements*, A.H. Smith, Eng. Place Name Soc., xxv, CUP 1956.
4 *A History of Wiltshire*, B. Watkin, Phillimore, 1989.
5 *Wiltshire Churches*, Parker & Chandler, Alan Sutton Pubs., 1993.
6 *Anglo-Saxon England*, F. M. Stenton, OUP 1947, pp. 432-5.
7 *An Atlas of Anglo-Saxon England*, D. Hill, Blackwell, 1981, p. 157.
8 Stenton p. 658.
9 All mileages from Hindon in this paper are by crow.
10 *Atlas of Anglo-Saxon England*, pp. 157–8.
11 *Place-names of Wiltshire*, Gower, Mawer & Stenton.
12 *VCH/Wilts.*, xi, 96.
13 The term 'manor' is anachronistic, but it conveys a reasonably accurate impression.
14 *Domesday Book, Wiltshire*, Phillimore, 1979.
15 *Anglo-Saxon England*, Stenton, p. 276.
16 *VCH/Wilts.*, ii, 182-3.
17 *Dictionary of National Biography (DNB).*
18 *Domesday Book to Magna Carta*, A.L. Poole, OUP,1951.
19 *The Thirteenth Century*, Sir M. Powicke, OUP, 1953.
20 *The Six New Towns of the Bishops of Winchester, 1200-55*, M. Beresford, Med. Arch., iii, 1959.
21 *VCH/Wilts.*, xi, 98.
22 *Six New Towns*, M. Beresford, p. 202.
23 *Domesday Book to Magna Carta*, A. L. Poole, p. 77.
24 On markets and fairs above, generally: *VCH/Wilts*, xi, 100-101; *Six New Towns*, Beresford, 200-202; *Endless Street*, John Chandler, The Hobnob Press, 1983.
25 *Calendar of Charter Rolls,* 1327-41, 258, Public Record Office (PRO).
26 *Wiltshire Archaeological Magazine (WAM)*, xii, 370, ref. 1553.
27 *Droving in Wiltshire: The Trade & its Routes*, K.G. Watts, Wiltshire Life Society, 1990.
28 *VCH/Wilts.*, xiii, 103.
29 *Salisbury & Wiltshire Journal*, 28th October, 1833.

30 Hampshire Record Office, Winchester, cat.11M59/B1/10.
31 *The Tropenell Cartulary*, ed. J S Davies, 1908.
32 *WAM*, xii, 370.
33 *VCH/Wilts.*, xi, 101.
34 *Calendar of Patent Rolls*, 1558, PRO.
35 *Register of John Waltham*, Canterbury & York Soc.
36 *VCH/Wilts.*, xi, 101.
37 *Cal. Pat.* 1549, PRO.
38 WAM xii, 370.
39 *WAM*, xxxvi, 531.
40 *Dictionary of Ecclesiastical Law*, Burn.
41 *Cal. Pat.* 1558, PRO.
42 *VCH/Wilts.*, xi, 95.
43 MSS records of Wilts. Quarter Sessions, pres. *Calendar of State Papers, Domestic*, 1635/6, PRO.
44 *WAM* xix, 196; xl, 308.
45 Wilts & Swindon Record Office (W&SRO), Trowbridge, cat. D1/54/1/3.
46 *Catholic Recusancy in Wiltshire, 1660-1791*. J.A. Williams, Cath. Record Soc., 1968.
47 *Wilts. Record Soc.* xxvii, ed. M. Ransome, 1971.
48 W&SRO, cat. 1730/9a.
49 *VCH/Wilts.*, viii, xi, xiii.
50 Report of Charity Commissioners, 1906.
51 W&SRO, cat. TA Hindon.
52 W&SRO, cat. 1730/18.
53 W&SRO, cat. 536/21.
54 *Church Briefs*, W. A. Bewes, 1896.
55 *Biog. Dict. of Eng. Architects 1600-1840*. H. Colvin, 3rd ed., 1995.
56 W&SRO, cat. 1730/9.
57 *The Buildings of England – Wiltshire*, 2nd ed. N. Pevsner & B. Cherry 1975.
58 W&SRO, cat. 1730/9.
59 *Salisbury Journal*.
60 W&SRO, cat. D1/56/7.
61 *VCH/Wilts.*, iii, 132-4. *Hist. of Hindon*, N. Sheard. H. Bull, notes. *A Century's Hist. of Wilts. & E. Somerset Congregational Union, 1797-1897*, S. B. Stribling, 1897.
62 H. Bull, notes. *Hist. of Hindon*, N. Sheard. *Western Gazette*, 13.5.1977.
63 W&SRO, cat. 1730/13.
64 *VCH/Wilts.*, viii, 60; xiii, 112-114.
65 *The Modern Hist. of S. Wiltshire*, Sir R. Colt Hoare, Bt., v.1, 1822, pp. 194, 227
66 *WAM* xxvii, 120, xlii, 200.
67 W&SRO cat. D1/61/21/12.
68 H. Bull, notes.
69 *History & Imagery in British Churches*, M.D. Anderson, John Murray, 1971 pp. 84, 134-5.
70 *Hist. of Hindon*, N. Sheard, p. 43.
71 *Buildings of Eng. – Wilts.*